Letts

KS2
Succe

Age
9-10

Mental arithmetic

Practice
workbook

09/17

15 MAR 2019

Paul
Broadbent

D0336949

About this book

Mental arithmetic

Mental arithmetic involves carrying out calculations and working with numbers in your head, without the help of a calculator or computer. It is an important part of your child's education in maths and will help them to manage everyday situations in later life. This book will help your child to solve increasingly difficult problems in their head and at greater speed. It provides the opportunity to learn, practise and check progress in a wide range of mental arithmetic skills, such as addition, subtraction, multiplication, division and working with fractions, decimals and measures. This book will also aid preparation for the **Key Stage 2 mathematics** test.

Features of the book

Learn and revise – explains and refreshes mental arithmetic skills and strategies.

Practice activities – a variety of tasks to see how well your child has grasped each skill.

Mental arithmetic tests – 20 questions which test and reinforce your child's understanding of the preceding topics.

Speed tests and *Progress charts* – the one-minute tests challenge your child to carry out mental calculations at increasing speed and the progress charts enable them to record their results.

Key facts – a summary of key points that your child should learn by heart and memorise.

Answers are in a pull-out booklet at the centre of the book.

Mental arithmetic tips

- Cooking with your child provides opportunities to use measures – reading scales, converting between units and calculating with amounts.

- Look at prices and compare amounts when shopping. Use receipts to find differences between prices.

- Play board games, such as a simplified version of *Monopoly*, and dice games, such as *Yahtzee*, taking opportunities to add and subtract numbers and money.

- Addition and subtraction facts to 20 and the multiplication tables are basic key facts that your child will need to know so that they can solve problems with bigger numbers. Regularly practise these facts – you could write them on sticky notes around the house for your child to see or answer.

- Short, regular practice to build confidence is better than spending too long on an activity so that boredom creeps in. Keep each session to 20–30 minutes.

Contents

Counting and numbers

Learn and revise

Look at the pattern in number sequences to continue them.

| 12 000 | 22 000 | 32 000 | 42 000 | _____ |

The next number is 52 000

You can also look at the difference between the numbers to work out the size of each step.

$$\overset{-7}{\frown}\ \overset{-7}{\frown}\ \overset{-7}{\frown}\ \overset{-7}{\frown}$$

725 718 711 704 ____

This is going down in sevens. The next number is 697.

When you count backwards past zero, you will use negative numbers. Picture them on a number line to help you see them in sequence.

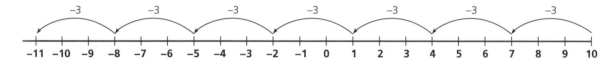

−11 −10 −9 −8 −7 −6 −5 −4 −3 −2 −1 0 1 2 3 4 5 6 7 8 9 10

Practice activities

1. Write the missing numbers in each sequence.

    a)   108   158   _____   258   _____   358   _____

    b)   _____   _____   6405   6505   6605   _____   6805

    c)   18   _____   4   −3   _____   _____   −24

    d)   7855   7825   7795   _____   _____   7705   _____

    e)   −35   −20   _____   _____   _____   40   55

2. Two numbers in each sequence have been swapped over.

Circle the two numbers.

a) 480   478   468   474   472   470   476

b) 3165   3150   3155   3160   3145   3170   3175

c) 1144   1124   1136   1132   1128   1140   1120

3. This is the halfway number between 2016 and 2032.

2016 ------ 2024 ------ 2032

What are these halfway numbers?

a) 42 440 ------ _____ ------ 42 880

b) −34 --------- _____ ------ −6

c) 60 038 ------ _____ ------ 61 038

d) 91 458 ------ _____ ------ 95 458

4. Count in these steps. Write the missing numbers.

a) Count in 10s:

48 760   _____   _____   _____   48 800

b) Count in 10s:

−27   _____   _____   _____   13

c) Count in 100s:

20 845   _____   _____   _____   21 245

d) Count in 100s:

43 959   _____   _____   _____   44 359

e) Count in 1000s:

37 008   _____   _____   _____   41 008

f) Count in 1000s:

98 255   _____   _____   _____   102 255

Place value

Look at this number and how it is made:

817 265 = 800 000 + 10 000 + 7000 + 200 + 60 + 5

eight hundred and seventeen thousand two hundred and sixty-five

Hundred thousands	Ten thousands	Thousands	Hundreds	Tens	Ones
8	1	7	2	6	5

800 000 > 10 000 > 7000 > 200 > 60 > 5 >

When you read large numbers, group the digits in threes starting with the ones digit. These are then easier to read:

340 285 ⟶ 340 *thousand* 285

Practice activities

1. Write the missing numbers.

   a) 72 195 = 70 000 + 2000 + _____ + _____ + _____

   b) 46 355 = _____ + _____ + _____ + 50 + 5

   c) 149 837 = 100 000 + _____ + _____ + _____ + 30 + _____

   d) 283 954 = _____ + _____ + _____ + _____ + _____ + 4

   e) 723 593 = _____ + 20 000 + _____ + _____ + _____ + _____

2. Write these as words.

   a) 23 456 _____

   _____

   b) 305 093 _____

   _____

6

3. Write down in words the value of the 2 digit in each number.

a) 72 483 _____

b) 248 660 _____

c) 492 863 _____

d) 820 357 _____

e) 295 780 _____

f) 372 009 _____

4. **a)** What number is 5000 more than 26 145? _____

b) What number is 10 000 more than 85 035? _____

c) What number is 50 000 less than 178 360? _____

d) What number is 20 000 less than 34 223? _____

5. Write these numbers as figures.

a) twenty-eight thousand two hundred and eight _____

b) four hundred and seven thousand two hundred _____

c) nine hundred thousand and six _____

d) six hundred and ninety thousand _____

e) one hundred and fifty-four thousand
seven hundred and thirty-one _____

f) two hundred thousand and seventy-three _____

6. Write the missing numbers for this multiplication machine.

IN	234		93		345
OUT		30 000		41 000	

Ordering and rounding numbers

Learn and revise

If you have a list of numbers to put in order, compare the place value of the digits in each number. Compare the largest value in each number and then the next largest, and so on.

Example: Put these in order, starting with the smallest.

189 456   17 432   190 355   18 045 ⟶ 17 432   18 045   189 456   190 355

Rounding makes numbers easier to work with – change them to the nearest 10, 100, 1000 or 10 000. It is useful for estimating approximate answers.

Rounding 38 465 to the nearest:

    10 is 38 470

    100 is 38 500

    1000 is 38 000

10 000 is 40 000

Practice activities

1. Write < or > to make these correct.

    a) 21 735 ____ 20 889   **b)** 53 478 ____ 53 521

    c) 61 350 ____ 62 007   **d)** 31 486 ____ 31 468

2. Underline the smallest number in this set. Draw a circle around the largest.

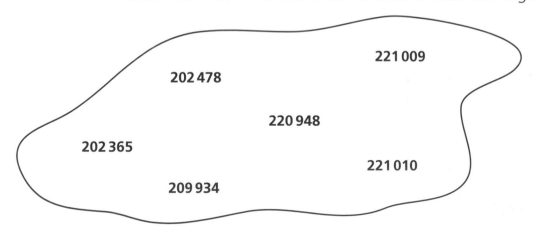

221 009
202 478
220 948
202 365
221 010
209 934

Ordering and rounding numbers

3. Write each set of numbers in order of size, starting with the smallest.

   a) 428 355   425 009   428 309   425 010

   _____   _____   _____   _____

   smallest

   b) 238 970   230 980   245 000   240 500

   _____   _____   _____   _____

   smallest

   c) 863 015   866 351   863 501   863 510

   _____   _____   _____   _____

   smallest

   d) 531 962   513 962   531 926   513 629

   _____   _____   _____   _____

   smallest

4. Round each of these numbers to the nearest 10.

   a) 6793   _____   b) 3586   _____

   c) 29 136   _____   d) 83 452   _____

   e) 276 834   _____   f) 579 356   _____

5. Round each of these numbers to the nearest 100.

   a) 2186   _____   b) 6754   _____

   c) 34 257   _____   d) 61 548   _____

   e) 843 956   _____   f) 286 541   _____

6. Round each of these numbers to the nearest 1000.

   a) 4845   _____   b) 7487   _____

   c) 36 404   _____   d) 43 529   _____

   e) 189 456   _____   f) 207 863   _____

Mental arithmetic test 1

1. Round each number to the nearest 10.

58 834 ⟶ _____

927 015 ⟶ _____

2. Write in words the value of the underlined digit.

4̲90 152

_____

3. Multiply both numbers by 1000.

26 _____

519 _____

4. Circle the smallest number and underline the largest number.

32 607   27 036   30 762

26 703   32 076

5. Write the halfway number.

−25   -------_____-------   −5

6. Write the missing number.

5195   5095   _____   4895   4795

7. Write two hundred and sixty-one thousand four hundred and ten as figures.

_____

8. What number is 6000 less than 988 799?

_____

9. Write the next number.

44 372   44 272   44 172   _____

10. Make the smallest possible number from these digit cards.

| 7 | | 8 | | 2 |

| | 1 | | 3 | |

▢▢▢▢▢

11. What number is 30 000 more than 214 503?

_____

12. Write < or > to make these correct.

895 135 _____ 895 513 _____ 893 555

13. Count in 1000s. Write the missing numbers.

58 820   _____   _____   61 820

14. Write the missing numbers.

−43   −23   _____   _____   37

15. Write in words the value of the underlined digit.

5̲706 289

_____

16. Round each number to the nearest 1000.

17 465 ⟶ _____

332 960 ⟶ _____

17. Write in words the value of the underlined digit.

917 2̲64

_____

18. Multiply both numbers by 100.

2054 _____

631 _____

19. Write < or > to make this correct.

46 743 _____ 467 343

20. Write the next two numbers.

18   10   2   _____   _____

Score   /20

10

Mental arithmetic test 2

1. Write in words the value of the underlined digit.

   9_70 480

   _____

2. Write < or > to make these correct.

   32 323 _____ 32 322

   675 707 _____ 767 507

3. What number is 2000 more than 541 045?

   _____

4. Make the largest possible number from these digit cards.

   | 3 | | 7 | | 8 |
   | | 0 | | 4 | | 1 |

   ⬚⬚⬚⬚⬚⬚

5. Count in 10s and write the missing numbers.

   –23 _____ _____ _____ 17

6. Multiply both numbers by 1000.

   68 _____

   984 _____

7. Write the next two numbers.

   14   9   4   _____   _____

8. Write the missing number.

   1465   1515 _____ 1615

9. Round each number to the nearest 100.

   8544 ⟶ _____

   210 766 ⟶ _____

10. Write five hundred and twelve thousand six hundred and twenty as figures.

    _____

11. Round each number to the nearest 1000.

    91 837 ⟶ _____

    552 400 ⟶ _____

12. What number is 40 000 less than 578 899?

    _____

13. Write the next number.

    37 204   38 204   39 204 _____

14. Write four hundred and ninety-one thousand two hundred and six as figures.

    _____

15. Write the halfway number.

    74 140 ------- _____ ------- 78 140

16. Multiply both numbers by 100.

    525 _____

    1903 _____

17. Write < or > to make this correct.

    328 154 _____ 38 210

18. Write in words the value of the underlined digit.

    3_16 758

    _____

19. Write the missing numbers.

    –12 _____ –2   3 _____

20. Circle the smallest number and underline the largest number.

    814 950   815 049   809 451

    804 591   815 409

Score /20

11

Addition

Learn and revise

Use any facts you know to help learn others.

8 + 6 = 14

You can use this to work out these and other facts:

18 + 16 = 34	80 + 60 = 140
1800 + 1600 = 3400	800 + 600 = 1400
4080 + 3060 = 7140	5008 + 1006 = 6014

Practice activities

1. Use the first answer to help with the others in each set.

a) 7 + 6 = _____

70 + 60 = _____   700 + 600 = _____

1007 + 3006 = _____   2070 + 4060 = _____

b) 9 + 5 = _____

90 + 50 = _____   900 + 500 = _____

49 + 25 = _____   1090 + 6050 = _____

c) 3 + 8 = _____

30 + 80 = _____   300 + 800 = _____

6300 + 2800 = _____   4030 + 3080 = _____

d) 8 + 7 = _____

80 + 70 = _____   800 + 700 = _____

58 + 37 = _____   3080 + 2070 = _____

2. Write the missing numbers on these addition walls. Each missing number is the sum of the two numbers below.

a)

b)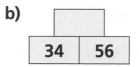

c)

d)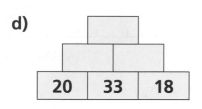

e)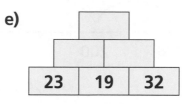

f)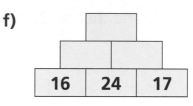

3. Look at these numbers and answer the questions.

1405   **2002**   **2404**   **3003**

a) Add together the two odd numbers.   _____

b) What is the total of the two smallest numbers? _____

c) Add together the two even numbers.   _____

d) What is the total of the two largest numbers? _____

e) Find the total of the three largest numbers.   _____

4. Look at these.

1234 + 8765 = 9999   **3333 + 6666 = 9999**

Find four more 4-digit additions that total 9999.

_____ + _____ = 9999

_____ + _____ = 9999

_____ + _____ = 9999

_____ + _____ = 9999

Subtraction

Learn and revise

There are different strategies you can use to subtract mentally.

Counting on from the smallest number is a good method.

Example: What is 320 subtract 170?

Count on from 170 to 200 and then to 320.

+30

+120

170   200   300   320

$$320 - 170 = 150$$

You could try breaking numbers up so that you can subtract them in your head.

Example: Take away 150 from 192.

$$192 - 150 =$$

$$190 + 2 - 150 =$$

$$190 - 150 + 2 = 40 + 2 = 42$$

Practice activities

1. Use the number lines to help you subtract these mentally.

    a)
    180 200   270

    $$270 - 180 = \underline{\hphantom{000}}$$

    b)
    240   300   410

    $$410 - 240 = \underline{\hphantom{000}}$$

    c)
    180   200   300   325

    $$325 - 180 = \underline{\hphantom{000}}$$

    d)
    250   300   345

    $$345 - 250 = \underline{\hphantom{000}}$$

    e)
    270   300   400   455

    $$455 - 270 = \underline{\hphantom{000}}$$

2. Answer these.

    a) Take 35 away from 92. _____

    b) Subtract 130 from 208. _____

    c) What is 49 less than 120? _____

    d) Take away 63 from 101. _____

    e) What is 121 take away 97? _____

3. Look at these numbers and answer the questions.

    1200   **3100**   **2800**   **3900**

    a) Which two numbers have a difference of 300?

        _____ and _____

    b) Which number is 100 less than 4000?

        _____

    c) Which two numbers have a difference of 1600?

        _____ and _____

4. Complete each chart to show the numbers coming out of each subtraction machine.

    a)

IN → −240 → OUT

IN	330	500	410	365	315	405
OUT	90					

    b)

IN → −380 → OUT

IN	570	640	410	500	730	620
OUT						

Addition and subtraction problems

Learn and revise

Look out for addition and subtraction words in any problems. They can give a clue for how to solve the problem.

Addition words	Subtraction words
add, total, altogether, sum, plus, more than, increase	subtract, take away, minus, less than, fewer, difference, reduce

Be careful though, some problems are confusing. Read them carefully and 'picture' the problem.

Practice activities

1. Answer these to find out how much is left for each one.

   a) A jug holds 1200 ml of orange juice. 750 ml is poured into one glass and 350 ml into another glass.

      How much orange juice is left? _____ ml

   b) Megan buys 5500 mm of cloth. She cuts off a piece 1400 mm long to make a skirt and cuts another piece of 2500 mm to make a scarf.

      How much cloth is left over? _____ mm

   c) Mrs Wise buys a 3200 g box of washing powder. She gives 1800 g to her sister and uses 900 g herself.

      How much washing powder is left in the box? _____ g

   e) A farmer collects 370 eggs one week and 420 the next week. He has to throw 35 away as they were cracked.

      How many eggs does he have left to take to market? _____

2. Two boxes of paper have a difference in weight of 3600 g. When they are put together, they have a total weight of 6400 g. What is the weight of each box of paper?

_____ g and _____ g

3. These are the lengths of some of the longest rivers in the world, rounded to the nearest 10 km. Answer the questions that follow.

River	Continent	Length
Nile	Africa	6690 km
Amazon	S. America	6380 km
Mississippi	N. America	6270 km
Chang Jiang	Asia	6210 km

a) What is the difference in length between the two longest rivers in the world, the Nile and the Amazon?

_____ km

b) Which river is 480 km shorter than the Nile? _____

c) Which two rivers have a difference in length of 420 km?

_____

4. A school is collecting bottle tops for recycling. It is aiming for a target of 3000 bottle tops. These are the totals for the first three months:

Month	Bottle tops collected
January	800
February	690
March	710

How many more bottle tops does the school need to collect to reach its target?

_____

Mental arithmetic test 3

1. 320 − 280 = _____

2. Answer these.

    40 + 70 = _____

    3400 + 2700 = _____

3. A school has 560 children. 285 are girls. How many boys are there?

    _____

4. What is 100 less than 6000?

    _____

5. What is the total of 1490 and 6204?

    _____

6. Take 45 away from 80. _____

7. Two parcels weigh 2800 g and 1300 g. What is the total weight of the parcels?

    _____ g

8. 56 + 28 = _____

    These are the amounts of water used by one person in one year. Use these amounts to answer 9–10.

    Daily normal shower = 2200 litres

    Daily power shower = 8030 litres

9. How much less water is used over a year using a normal shower than a power shower?

    _____ litres

10. How much water would two people use over a year if they had a normal shower every day?

    _____ litres

11. Circle the odd one out.

    6473 + 1304   5281 + 3607

    2764 + 5013   4025 + 3752

12. What is 108 take away 94?

    _____

13. 415 − 350 = _____

14. 3008 + 2005 = _____

15. 1450 ml of milk is used from a 2500 ml jug. How much milk is left in the jug?

    _____ ml

16. Add together 2003, 5406 and 1401.

    _____

17. Circle two numbers that have a difference of 1500.

    6500   7200

    5700   6200   5100

18. 430 − 280 = _____

19. 27 + 43 = _____

20. A train travels 635 km from London to Edinburgh. How far is the return journey there and back again?

    _____ km

Score   /20

Mental arithmetic test 4

1. 37 + 39 = _____

2. Circle two numbers that have a difference of 400.

   3200   3900
   4100   3700   4200

3. 440 – 170 = _____

4. Circle the odd one out.

   4725 + 4163   1208 + 7680
      3561 + 5217   2353 + 6535

5. Two of the highest mountains in Britain are Ben Nevis at 1344 m and Snowdon at 1085 m. How much higher is Ben Nevis than Snowdon?

   _____ m

6. Take 32 away from 100. _____

7. 305 – 203 = _____

8. Answer these.

   90 + 20 = _____

   5900 + 2200 = _____

   Look at these numbers for 9–10.

   3501   1500   2425   4030

9. What is the difference between the largest and the smallest number?

   _____

10. What is the total of the two odd numbers?

   _____

11. 4060 + 3060 = _____

12. Subtract 76 from 110. _____

13. There are 350 pages in a book. Sam read 75 pages at school and another 60 pages at home. How many more pages are left for Sam to read?

   _____

14. 45 + 35 = _____

15. A cake is made with 350 g flour, 175 g butter and 140 g sugar. What is the total weight of the cake?

   _____ g

16. Add together 2380 and 5107.

   _____

17. What is 10 less than 2000?

   _____

18. It is 1460 m from Jo's house to school. She walks to school and back home every day. How far in total does she walk each day?

   _____ m

19. 625 – 250 = _____

20. What is the total of these three numbers?

   2303   5005   1605

   _____

Multiples, factors and primes

Learn and revise

A **multiple** of a whole number is produced by multiplying that number by another whole number.

Multiples of 3 ⟶	3	6	9	12	15	18...	60...	300...
	×1	×2	×3	×4	×5	×6...	×20...	×100...
Multiples of 4 ⟶	4	8	12	16	20	24...	80...	400...

12 is a multiple of both 3 and 4.

This means that 12 is a **common multiple** of 3 and 4.

Factors of a number can divide that number exactly.

Factors of 18:

18 = 1 × 18   18 = 2 × 9   18 = 3 × 6

In order: 1, 2, 3, 6, 9, 18

In pairs: (1, 18), (2, 9), (3, 6)

A **prime number** has only two factors: 1 and itself.

2, 3, 5, 7 and 11 are the first five prime numbers.

Practice activities

1. Write the numbers in the correct part of this Venn diagram.

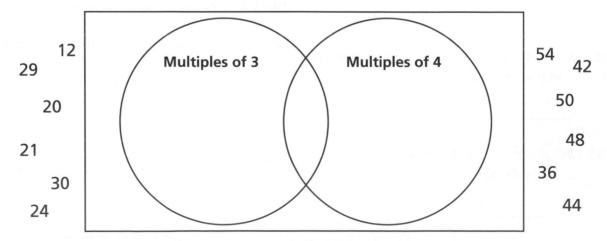

Multiples, factors and primes

2. Circle the correct answer for each of these.

    a) A common multiple of 3 and 5 is: **b)** A common multiple of 2 and 3 is:

        35   45   55   28   38   48

    c) A common multiple of 5 and 6 is: **d)** A common multiple of 3 and 10 is:

        70   80   90   100   120   160

3. Write the factors of these numbers in pairs.

    a) 27 _____

    b) 60 _____

    c) 42 _____

    d) 48 _____

4. Use these numbers to answer each question.

                                            12   8

    a) Which number is a factor of 64?   ____

    b) Which number is a factor of 35?   ____   9   5

    c) Which two numbers are factors of 36? ____ and ____

    d) Which two numbers are factors of 60? ____ and ____

5. Find the factors of these prime numbers and square numbers.

    a) Write the factors for each number in order.

Prime numbers	**Square numbers**
19 _____	16 _____
23 _____	9 _____
5 _____	25 _____
37 _____	36 _____

    b) What do you notice about the number of factors for prime numbers?

        _____

    c) What do you notice about the number of factors for square numbers?

        _____

Multiplication

Use the tables facts that you know to help you multiply bigger numbers.

$$8 \times 4 = 32$$

$$80 \times 40 = 3200$$

Partition numbers and mentally calculate each part to make them easier to work with.

Follow these steps to answer 83 multiplied by 4:

83×4 is the same as 80×4 added to 3×4

$$320 + 12 = 332$$

So $83 \times 4 = 332$

Practice activities

1. Answer these.

   a) 7×9 = _____

   70×90 = _____

   b) 6×3 = _____

   60×30 = _____

   c) 8×6 = _____

   80×60 = _____

   d) 9×9 = _____

   90×90 = _____

   e) 7×8 = _____

   70×80 = _____

   f) 9×12 = _____

   90×120 = _____

2. Complete this multiplication grid.

×	32	54	45
6			
3			
8			

3. Answer these.

a) 46 × 3 = _____

b) 39 × 5 = _____

c) 28 × 6 = _____

d) 54 × 4 = _____

e) 81 × 3 = _____

f) 65 × 8 = _____

4. Multiply these sets of three numbers.

a)
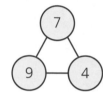

_____

b)
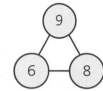

_____

c)

_____

d)
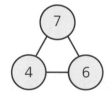

_____

5. Use these digits.

5 **6** **9**

Arrange the three digits to make multiplications like this:

9 **6** × **5** =

a) Arrange the digits to make the largest product.

⬜⬜ × ⬜ = _____

b) Arrange the digits to make the smallest product.

⬜⬜ × ⬜ = _____

c) Arrange the digits to make the product as close as possible to 500.

⬜⬜ × ⬜ = _____

Division

Learn and revise

Break numbers up to help you work out division answers.

Example: What is 94 divided by 4?

Break 94 up into 80 and 14.

$$80 \div 4 = 20$$
$$14 \div 4 = 3 \text{ r } 2$$
$$\text{So } 94 \div 4 = 23 \text{ r } 2$$

When there is a remainder it can be represented in different ways.

$94 \div 4 = 23 \text{ r } 2$ or... $94 \div 4 = 23\frac{1}{2}$ or... $94 \div 4 = 23.5$

Practice activities

1. Write the missing numbers. Use your multiplication and division facts to help you answer each one.

   a) $27 \div \boxed{} = 3$

   b) $28 \div 4 = \boxed{}$

   c) $\boxed{} \div 9 = 4$

   d) $24 \div 8 = \boxed{}$

   e) $49 \div \boxed{} = 7$

   f) $\boxed{} \div 3 = 6$

   g) $27 \div 9 = \boxed{}$

   h) $54 \div \boxed{} = 6$

   i) $56 \div 7 = \boxed{}$

   j) $\boxed{} \div 12 = 8$

   k) $110 \div 11 = \boxed{}$

   l) $\boxed{} \div 6 = 12$

2. Answer these.

a) 96 ÷ 4 = _____   **b)** 105 ÷ 5 = _____

c) 93 ÷ 3 = _____   **d)** 84 ÷ 6 = _____

e) 112 ÷ 7 = _____   **f)** 112 ÷ 4 = _____

g) 126 ÷ 6 = _____   **h)** 153 ÷ 3 = _____

3. Answer these and show the remainders in three different ways.

a) 47 ÷ 4 = _____ or _____ or _____

b) 83 ÷ 5 = _____ or _____ or _____

c) 91 ÷ 2 = _____ or _____ or _____

d) 97 ÷ 10 = _____ or _____ or _____

e) 69 ÷ 4 = _____ or _____ or _____

f) 99 ÷ 5 = _____ or _____ or _____

4. Complete each chart with the numbers coming out of each division machine.

a)

IN → ÷11 → OUT

IN	1100	3300	7700	9900	11 000	13 200
OUT	100					

b)

IN → ÷12 → OUT

IN	4800	2400	6000	9600	12 000	14 400
OUT						

Mental arithmetic test 5

1. What is the next prime number after 13?

   _____

2. $49 \div 7 =$ _____

3. Write the missing pair of factors for 18.

   (1, 18) (2, 9) (_____ , _____)

4. Answer these.

   $9 \times 6 =$ _____

   $90 \times 60 =$ _____

5. $28 \times 5 =$ _____

6. Answer this, writing the remainder as a decimal.

   $55 \div 2 =$ _____

7. $8800 \div 11 =$ _____

8. Circle the number that is **not** a prime number.

   21   41

   11   31

9. Write the missing factor for 16.

   1, 2, _____ , 8, 16

10. $40 \times 70 =$ _____

11. Circle the number that is a common multiple of 5 and 3.

    40

   70   60

12. $36 \div 12 =$ _____

13. $53 \times 7 =$ _____

14. What is the remainder when 58 is divided by 6?

    r = _____

15. Write < or > to make this correct.

    8×24 _____ 2×84

16. Multiply these three numbers.

    | 8 | 3 | 5 |

    _____

17. Answer this, writing the remainder as a fraction.

    $72 \div 5 =$ _____

    Look at these numbers for 18–20.

    4   8   5   12

18. Which number is a multiple of 3? _____

19. Which number is **not** a factor of 60?

    _____

20. Which number is a factor of 52? _____

Score   /20

26

Mental arithmetic test 6

1. $55 \div 11 =$ _____

2. Answer these.

   $8 \times 9 =$ _____

   $80 \times 90 =$ _____

3. What is the remainder when 45 is divided by 6?

   r = _____

4. Circle the number that is a common multiple of 2 and 4.

   28

   18   38

5. $56 \div 8 =$ _____

6. $37 \times 5 =$ _____

7. Multiply these three numbers.

     4 **7** **6**

   _____

8. $80 \times 30 =$ _____

9. Answer this, writing the remainder as a fraction.

   $93 \div 10 =$ _____

10. Write the missing pair of factors for 30.

    (1, 30) (2, 15) (3, 10) (_____, _____)

11. What is the next prime number after 19?

    _____

12. Answer this, writing the remainder as a decimal.

    $50 \div 4 =$ _____

13. $63 \times 7 =$ _____

14. Write < or > to make this correct.

    9×34 _____ 4×93

15. $24 \div 12 =$ _____

16. Write the missing factor for 36.

    1, 2, 3, 4, _____, 9, 12, 18, 36

17. Circle the number that is **not** a prime number.

    23   43

    13   33

    Look at these numbers for 18–20.

    12   9   6   7

18. Which number is a multiple of 4? _____

19. Which number is **not** a factor of 36?

    _____

20. Which number is a factor of 45?

    _____

Score   /20

27

Fractions

Learn and revise

Proper fractions

If the numerator is smaller than the denominator, it is known as a **proper fraction**. The value of each fraction is less than 1, e.g.

$$\frac{1}{6} \qquad \frac{3}{4} \qquad \frac{7}{10}$$

Improper fractions

If the numerator is larger than the denominator, it is known as an **improper fraction**. The value of each fraction is greater than 1, e.g.

$$\frac{3}{2} \qquad \frac{7}{4} \qquad \frac{10}{7}$$

This shows seven slices of melon. Each slice is $\frac{1}{4}$ of a whole melon.

There is one whole melon and $\frac{3}{4}$ of a melon.

$\frac{4}{4} + \frac{3}{4} = \frac{7}{4}$ or $1\frac{3}{4}$

$\frac{7}{4}$ is an improper fraction. $1\frac{3}{4}$ is a mixed number.

Practice activities

1. Write these as mixed numbers and improper fractions.

a)

Mixed number: _____

Improper fraction: _____

b)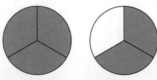

Mixed number: _____

Improper fraction: _____

c)

Mixed number: _____

Improper fraction: _____

d)

Mixed number: _____

Improper fraction: _____

2. Change these mixed numbers to improper fractions.

a) $2\frac{1}{4}$ = ___ **b)** $4\frac{1}{3}$ = ___

c) $1\frac{5}{8}$ = ___ **d)** $3\frac{3}{4}$ = ___

e) $2\frac{2}{5}$ = ___ **f)** $1\frac{1}{6}$ = ___

3. Change these improper fractions to mixed numbers.

a) $\frac{3}{2}$ = ___ **b)** $\frac{5}{4}$ = ___

c) $\frac{10}{3}$ = ___ **d)** $\frac{8}{7}$ = ___

e) $\frac{15}{2}$ = ___ **f)** $\frac{16}{3}$ = ___

4. Write the fraction each arrow points to, as a mixed number and an improper fraction.

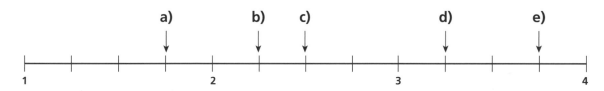

a) = ___ or ___ **b)** = ___ or ___

c) = ___ or ___ **d)** = ___ or ___

e) = ___ or ___

5. Write these in order, starting with the smallest.

$\frac{14}{4}$ $3\frac{3}{4}$ $\frac{12}{4}$ $2\frac{1}{4}$ $4\frac{1}{2}$ $\frac{11}{2}$

___ ___ ___ ___ ___ ___

smallest

Fractions of amounts

Learn and revise

Here are 20 oranges.

Which would give you the greatest number of oranges?

$\frac{1}{5}$ of 20	$\frac{1}{2}$ of 20	$\frac{1}{4}$ of 20
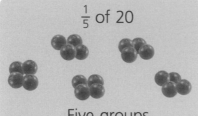	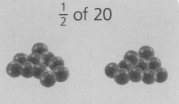	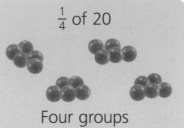
Five groups	Two groups	Four groups
$\frac{1}{5}$ of 20 = 4	$\frac{1}{2}$ of 20 = 10	$\frac{1}{4}$ of 20 = 5

$\frac{1}{2}$ is greater than $\frac{1}{4}$ and $\frac{1}{4}$ is greater than $\frac{1}{5}$. $\frac{1}{2} > \frac{1}{4} > \frac{1}{5}$

Practice activities

1. Circle the fraction that gives the largest amount. Use the pictures to help.

   a) 18 balls

   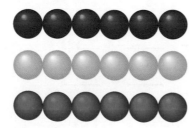

   $\frac{1}{6}$ $\frac{1}{3}$

   b) 16 balls

   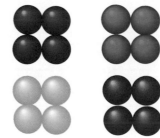

   $\frac{1}{4}$ $\frac{1}{2}$

   c) 21 balls

   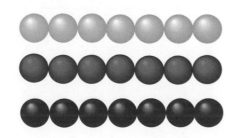

   $\frac{1}{3}$ $\frac{1}{7}$

   d) 18 balls

   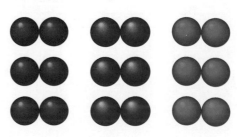

   $\frac{1}{6}$ $\frac{1}{9}$

Answers

Pages 4–5
1. a) 208, 308, 408   b) 6205, 6305, 6705
    c) 11, −10, −17   d) 7765, 7735, 7675
    e) −5, 10, 25
2. a) 468, 476   b) 3165, 3145   c) 1124, 1140
3. a) 42 660   b) −20   c) 60 538   d) 93 458
4. a) 48 770, 48 780, 48 790   b) −17, −7, 3
    c) 20 945, 21 045, 21 145   d) 44 059, 44 159, 44 259
    e) 38 008, 39 008, 40 008   f) 99 255, 100 255, 101 255

Pages 6–7
1. a) 100, 90, 5
    b) 40 000, 6000, 300
    c) 40 000, 9000, 800, 7
    d) 200 000, 80 000, 3000, 900, 50
    e) 700 000, 3000, 500, 90, 3
2. a) twenty-three thousand four hundred and fifty-six
    b) three hundred and five thousand and ninety-three
3. a) two thousand   b) two hundred thousand
    c) two thousand   d) twenty thousand
    e) two hundred thousand   f) two thousand
4. a) 31 145   b) 95 035   c) 128 360   d) 14 223
5. a) 28 208   b) 407 200   c) 900 006
    d) 690 000   e) 154 731   f) 200 073
6. Top row should be completed as follows: 30, 41
    Bottom row should be completed as follows:
    234 000, 93 000, 345 000

Pages 8–9
1. a) >   b) <   c) <   d) >
2. 202 365, (221 010)
3. a) 425 009, 425 010, 428 309, 428 355
    b) 230 980, 238 970, 240 500, 245 000
    c) 863 015, 863 501, 863 510, 866 351
    d) 513 629, 513 962, 531 926, 531 962
4. a) 6790   b) 3590   c) 29 140
    d) 83 450   e) 276 830   f) 579 360
5. a) 2200   b) 6800   c) 34 300
    d) 61 500   e) 844 000   f) 286 500
6. a) 5000   b) 7000   c) 36 000
    d) 44 000   e) 189 000   f) 208 000

Page 10
1. 58 830, 927 020   2. four hundred thousand
3. 26 000, 519 000   4. (26 703,) 32 607
5. −15   6. 4995
7. 261 410   8. 982 799
9. 44 072   10. 12 378
11. 244 503   12. <, >
13. 59 820, 60 820   14. −3, 17
15. seven hundred thousand   16. 17 000, 333 000
17. seven thousand   18. 205 400, 63 100
19. <   20. −6, −14

Page 11
1. nine hundred thousand   2. >, <
3. 543 045   4. 874 310
5. −13, −3, 7   6. 68 000, 984 000
7. −1, −6   8. 1565
9. 8500, 210 800   10. 512 620
11. 92 000, 552 000   12. 538 899
13. 40 204   14. 491 206
15. 76 140   16. 52 500, 190 300
17. >   18. six thousand
19. −7, 8   20. (804 591,) 815 409

Pages 12–13
1. a) 13, 130, 1300, 4013, 6130
    b) 14, 140, 1400, 74, 7140
    c) 11, 110, 1100, 9100, 7110
    d) 15, 150, 1500, 95, 5150

2. a) 64   b) 90   c) 81   d) 104, 53, 51
    e) 93, 42, 51   f) 81, 40, 41
3. a) 4408   b) 3407   c) 4406   d) 5407
    e) 7409
4. There are many possible answers. Check all additions
    total 9999.

Pages 14–15
1. a) 90   b) 170   c) 145   d) 95   e) 185
2. a) 57   b) 78   c) 71   d) 38   e) 24
3. a) 3100 and 2800   b) 3900   c) 1200 and 2800
4. a) Bottom row should be completed as follows:
    260, 170, 125, 75, 165
    b) Bottom row should be completed as follows:
    190, 260, 30, 120, 350, 240

Pages 16–17
1. a) 100 ml   b) 1600 mm   c) 500 g   d) 755
2. 1400 g and 5000 g
3. a) 310 km   b) Chang Jiang
    c) Nile and Mississippi
4. 800

Page 18
1. 40   2. 110, 6100
3. 275   4. 5900
5. 7694   6. 35
7. 4100 g   8. 84
9. 5830 litres   10. 4400 litres
11. 5281 + 3607   12. 14
13. 65   14. 5013
15. 1050 ml   16. 8810
17. 5700 and 7200   18. 150
19. 70   20. 1270 km

Page 19
1. 76   2. 3700 and 4100
3. 270   4. 3561 + 5217
5. 259 m   6. 68
7. 102   8. 110, 8100
9. 2530   10. 5926
11. 7120   12. 34
13. 215   14. 80
15. 665 g   16. 7487
17. 1990   18. 2920 m
19. 375   20. 8913

Pages 20–21
1.

2. a) 45   b) 48   c) 90   d) 120
3. a) (1, 27) (3, 9)
    b) (1, 60) (2, 30) (3, 20) (4, 15) (5, 12) (6, 10)
    c) (1, 42) (2, 21) (3, 14) (6, 7)
    d) (1, 48) (2, 24) (3, 16) (4, 12) (6, 8)
4. a) 8   b) 5   c) 12, 9   d) 12, 5
5. a) **Prime numbers:**
    19 → 1, 19; 23 → 1, 23;
    5 → 1, 5; 37 → 1, 37
    Square numbers:
    16 → 1, 2, 4, 8, 16
    9 → 1, 3, 9

Answers

25 → 1, 5, 25
36 → 1, 2, 3, 4, 6, 9, 12, 18, 36
b) There are only two factors.
c) There are an odd number of factors.

Pages 22–23
1. a) 63, 6300   b) 18, 1800   c) 48, 4800
   d) 81, 8100   e) 56, 5600   f) 108, 10800
2.

×	32	54	45
6	192	324	270
3	96	162	135
8	256	432	360

3. a) 138   b) 195   c) 168   d) 216
   e) 243   f) 520
4. a) 252   b) 240   c) 432   d) 168
5. a) $65 \times 9 = 585$ b) $69 \times 5 = 345$ c) $56 \times 9 = 504$

Pages 24–25
1. a) 9 b) 7 c) 36 d) 3 e) 7 f) 18
   g) 3 h) 9 i) 8 j) 96 k) 10 l) 72
2. a) 24 b) 21 c) 31 d) 14 e) 16
   f) 28 g) 21 h) 51
3. a) 11 r 3 or $11\frac{3}{4}$ or 11.75   b) 16 r 3 or $16\frac{3}{5}$ or 16.6
   c) 45 r 1 or $45\frac{1}{2}$ or 45.5   d) 9 r 7 or $9\frac{7}{10}$ or 9.7
   e) 17 r 1 or $17\frac{1}{4}$ or 17.25   f) 19 r 4 or $19\frac{4}{5}$ or 19.8
4. a) Bottom row should be completed as follows:
      300, 700, 900, 1000, 1200
   b) Bottom row should be completed as follows:
      400, 200, 500, 800, 1000, 1200

Page 26
1. 17   2. 7   3. (3, 6)   4. 54, 5400
5. 140   6. 27.5   7. 800   8. 21
9. 4   10. 2800   11. 60   12. 3
13. 371   14. 4   15. >   16. 120
17. $14\frac{2}{5}$ 18. 12   19. 8   20. 4

Page 27
1. 5   2. 72, 7200   3. 3   4. 28
5. 7   6. 185   7. 168   8. 2400
9. $9\frac{3}{10}$ 10. (5, 6)   11. 23   12. 12.5
13. 441   14. <   15. 2   16. 6
17. 33   18. 12   19. 7   20. 9

Pages 28–29
1. a) $1\frac{2}{3}, \frac{5}{3}$ b) $3\frac{1}{2}, \frac{7}{2}$ c) $2\frac{2}{5}, \frac{12}{5}$ d) $2\frac{1}{6}, \frac{13}{6}$
2. a) $\frac{9}{4}$ b) $\frac{13}{3}$ c) $\frac{13}{8}$ d) $\frac{15}{4}$
   e) $\frac{12}{5}$ f) $\frac{7}{6}$
3. a) $1\frac{1}{2}$ b) $1\frac{1}{4}$ c) $3\frac{1}{3}$ d) $1\frac{1}{7}$
   e) $7\frac{1}{2}$ f) $5\frac{1}{4}$
4. a) $1\frac{3}{4}, \frac{7}{4}$ b) $2\frac{1}{4}, \frac{9}{4}$ c) $2\frac{1}{2}, \frac{5}{2}$ d) $3\frac{1}{4}, \frac{13}{4}$
   e) $3\frac{3}{4}, \frac{15}{4}$
5. $2\frac{1}{4}, \frac{12}{4}, \frac{14}{4}, 3\frac{3}{4}, 4\frac{1}{2}, \frac{11}{2}$

Pages 30–31
1. a) $\frac{1}{3}$ b) $\frac{1}{2}$
   c) $\frac{1}{3}$ d) $\frac{1}{6}$
2. a) <   b) <
   c) >   d) <
3. a) $\frac{1}{2}, \frac{1}{5}, \frac{1}{10}, \frac{1}{4}, \frac{3}{4}$ b) $\frac{1}{10}, \frac{1}{2}, \frac{1}{4}, \frac{3}{4}, \frac{1}{5}$
   c) $\frac{1}{4}, \frac{1}{2}, \frac{1}{10}, \frac{3}{4}, \frac{1}{5}$
4. a) $\frac{1}{10}$ of 10 kg   b) thirds
   c) more time sleeping   d) more spotted fish

Pages 32–33
1. $1\frac{3}{4} \rightarrow 1\frac{1}{4}$ $2\frac{3}{10} \rightarrow \frac{7}{10}$ $1\frac{7}{8} \rightarrow 1\frac{1}{8}$
   $2\frac{1}{3} \rightarrow \frac{2}{3}$ $1\frac{1}{3} \rightarrow 1\frac{2}{3}$

2. a) $\frac{8}{4}$ (or 2)   b) $\frac{6}{10}$ (or $\frac{3}{5}$)   c) $\frac{9}{5}$ (or $1\frac{4}{5}$)   d) $\frac{8}{10}$ (or $\frac{4}{5}$)
3. a) $\frac{6}{4}$ or $1\frac{1}{2}$ b) $\frac{7}{6}$ or $1\frac{1}{6}$ c) $\frac{11}{10}$ or $1\frac{1}{10}$ d) $\frac{6}{5}$ or $1\frac{1}{5}$
4. a) $\frac{1}{2}$ or $\frac{2}{4}$ b) $\frac{3}{5}$ c) $\frac{7}{10}$ d) $\frac{2}{3}$
5. a) 7   b) $\frac{6}{10}$ m (or $\frac{3}{5}$ m)   c) $6\frac{1}{5}$ d) $2\frac{3}{10}$ litres
   e) $8\frac{1}{2}$ (or $8\frac{2}{4}$)

Page 34
1. 4   2. $\frac{1}{4}$
3. $1\frac{1}{2}$ and $3\frac{1}{2}$ 4. $\frac{9}{4}, 2\frac{1}{4}$
5. $\frac{11}{4}$ (or $2\frac{3}{4}$)   6. $\frac{27}{10}$
7. ($1\frac{1}{3}$) $\frac{8}{3}$ 8. 5
9. $\frac{1}{10} < \frac{1}{7} < \frac{1}{4} < \frac{1}{2}$ 10. $1\frac{4}{5}, \frac{9}{5}$
11. $\frac{7}{6}$ or $1\frac{1}{6}$ 12. 9
13. $\frac{7}{9}$ 14. 20p
15. $\frac{5}{2}, 2\frac{1}{2}$ 16. $\frac{14}{9}$ or $1\frac{5}{9}$
17. more blue balloons   18. $1\frac{2}{3}$
19. 84   20. <

Page 35
1. $\frac{8}{5}, 1\frac{3}{5}$ 2. 5
3. 8   4. 50p
5. $3\frac{1}{2}$ 6. more apples
7. <   8. $\frac{5}{8}$
9. $1\frac{2}{3}, \frac{5}{3}$ 10. $\frac{9}{8}$ or $1\frac{1}{8}$
11. ($\frac{8}{5}$) $2\frac{3}{5}$ 12. $\frac{4}{7}$
13. 45   14. $1\frac{3}{4}, 2\frac{1}{4}$
15. $\frac{1}{10}$ 16. $\frac{13}{10}$
17. $\frac{1}{8} < \frac{1}{6} < \frac{1}{5} < \frac{1}{3}$ 18. $\frac{11}{9}$ or $1\frac{2}{9}$
19. $\frac{7}{4}, 1\frac{3}{4}$ 20. 35

Pages 36–37
1. a) 3.4   b) 86   c) 12.28   d) 8.55
   e) 37.2   f) 16.2
2. a) 368   b) 30   c) 100.5   d) 293.4
   e) 65.5   f) 4638.5
3. a) 8.35   b) 1.9   c) 22.76   d) 2.845
   e) 0.093   f) 1.284
4. a) 0.27   b) 3.42
   c) 0.538   d) 0.063
   e) 0.279   f) 1.452
5. 0.855 kg, 0.95 kg, 8.245 kg, 8.3 kg, 8.455 kg, 8.52 kg
6. a) 3.3   b) 3.8   c) 3.1   d) 3.6
   e) 3.9   f) 3.4

Pages 38–39
1. a) 50%   b) 25%   c) 10%   d) 20%
   e) 60%   f) 72%   g) 58%   h) 65%
   i) 80%   j) 30%   k) 34%   l) 55%
2. a) $\frac{1}{10}$ b) $\frac{4}{5}$ c) $\frac{1}{2}$ d) $\frac{3}{10}$
   e) $\frac{3}{5}$ f) $\frac{1}{4}$ g) $\frac{1}{20}$ h) $\frac{9}{10}$
   i) $\frac{3}{4}$ j) $\frac{2}{5}$ k) $\frac{7}{10}$ l) $\frac{1}{100}$
3. a) 20%   b) 15%   c) 35%   d) 60%
   e) 50%   f) 30%   g) 75%   h) 90%
   i) 85%   j) 10%   k) 5%   l) 70%
4. a) 0.3   b) 0.45   c) 0.65   d) 0.8
   e) 0.9   f) 0.25   g) 0.05   h) 0.15
   i) 0.3   j) 0.55   k) 0.35   l) 0.85
5. a) 15%, 20%, 25%, $\frac{9}{25}$, $\frac{6}{10}$, $\frac{4}{5}$
   b) 10%, $\frac{1}{4}$, 40%, $\frac{23}{50}$, 60%, $\frac{7}{10}$
   c) $\frac{1}{50}$, 3%, $\frac{1}{10}$, $\frac{3}{20}$, 16%, 50%

Pages 40–41
1. $0.8 \times 3 \rightarrow 2.4$; $2.4 \times 6 \rightarrow 14.4$; $1.4 \times 9 \rightarrow 12.6$;
   $2.3 \times 8 \rightarrow 18.4$; $4.1 \times 5 \rightarrow 20.5$; $0.9 \times 5 \rightarrow 4.5$;
   $1.8 \times 6 \rightarrow 10.8$
2. a) 4.5   b) 3.6   c) 5.6   d) 9.2
   e) 7.1   f) 10.3
3. a) 4.4   b) 0.8   c) 5.4   d) 1.4
   e) 2.5   f) 4.8
4. $0.3 \times 6 = 1.8$; $3.4 \times 7 = 23.8$; $1.9 \times 5 = 9.5$; $2.6 \times 4 = 10.4$

Answers

Page 42
1.	50%	**2.**	13.6
3.	54.32	**4.**	(24%), $\frac{7}{25}$
5.	$\frac{3}{10}$	**6.**	0.8, $\frac{4}{5}$
7.	<	**8.**	0.73
9.	12.8	**10.**	(5.29 kg,) 0.925 kg
11.	>	**12.**	90%
13.	87	**14.**	4.2, 4 (or 4.0)
15.	2.8	**16.**	0.12
17.	0.65	**18.**	6.19
19.	1.5, 1.6	**20.**	0.5

Page 43
1.	$\frac{3}{4}$	**2.**	1.96
3.	700.4	**4.**	4.8
5.	2.8, 2.1	**6.**	1.9
7.	5.7	**8.**	4.5
9.	45%	**10.**	>
11.	(25%), $\frac{7}{20}$		
12.	3.8	**13.**	25%
14.	824	**15.**	1.093
16.	>	**17.**	11.1
18.	(3.05 kg,) 0.532 kg		
19.	0.34	**20.**	0.7

Pages 44–45

1.
a)	64	**b)**	121
c)	49	**d)**	36
e)	81	**f)**	100
g)	25	**h)**	144

2. The square numbers are all in a diagonal line.

3.
a) 4	**b)** 9	**c)** 16	**d)** 25
e) 36	**f)** 49	**g)** 64	**h)** 81
i) 100			

4. They are all square numbers.

Pages 46–47

1.
a)	15 cm², 16 cm	**b)**	24 cm², 20 cm
c)	25 cm², 20 cm	**d)**	18 cm², 18 cm
e)	36 cm², 24 cm	**f)**	32 cm², 24 cm

2. Area column should be completed as follows:
36, 40, 48, 49, 40, 45, 52, 100, 54, 121, 64, 400
Perimeter column should be completed as follows:
30, 28, 28, 28, 26, 36, 34, 50, 42, 44, 40, 80

3. **a)** 4 cm **b)** 16 cm
4. **a)** 9 cm **b)** 81 cm²

Pages 48–49

1.
a)	6.05 p.m.	**b)**	9.15 a.m.	**c)**	10.30 a.m.
d)	3.35 p.m.	**e)**	8.55 p.m.		

2.
a)	8.15 a.m.	**b)**	1 hour 45 minutes (or 1$\frac{3}{4}$ hours)
c)	4 hours 50 minutes	**d)**	11.50 a.m.
e)	6.15 a.m.		

3. **a)** Bus D **b)** Bus B

Page 50
1.	16	**2.**	12 m²
3.	4.05 p.m.	**4.**	Area = 32 cm²; Perimeter = 24 cm
5.	1 hour 25 minutes	**6.**	7 cm
7.	11.40 a.m.	**8.**	81
9.	80 cm	**10.**	10 cm
11.	36	**12.**	1 hour 40 minutes
13.	Area = 27 cm²; Perimeter = 24 cm	**14.**	6.10 p.m.
15.	144	**16.**	8 cm
17.	25	**18.**	Saturday
19.	45 minutes	**20.**	Sunday

Page 51
1.	Area = 21 cm²; Perimeter = 20 cm	**2.**	49
3.	1.15 p.m.	**4.**	3 cm
5.	6.55 p.m.	**6.**	64
7.	54 m²	**8.**	Sunday
9.	1 hour 25 minutes	**10.**	Saturday
11.	10 m	**12.**	7.55 a.m.
13.	6.20 p.m.	**14.**	9 cm
15.	121	**16.**	45 minutes
17.	16	**18.**	Area = 72 cm²; Perimeter = 34 cm
19.	2 hours 10 minutes	**20.**	25

Page 52
1.	90	**2.**	17
3.	20	**4.**	7
5.	7	**6.**	21
7.	50	**8.**	16
9.	50	**10.**	200
11.	90	**12.**	23
13.	300	**14.**	$\frac{4}{5}$
15.	140	**16.**	18
17.	900	**18.**	0.8
19.	3	**20.**	15
21.	110	**22.**	100
23.	13	**24.**	4
25.	13	**26.**	20
27.	0.5	**28.**	4
29.	9	**30.**	6
31.	90	**32.**	25
33.	$\frac{3}{5}$	**34.**	15
35.	5	**36.**	130
37.	22	**38.**	22
39.	22	**40.**	60

Page 54
1.	30	**2.**	32
3.	5	**4.**	2
5.	18	**6.**	60
7.	5	**8.**	5
9.	18	**10.**	10
11.	20	**12.**	24
13.	120	**14.**	4
15.	42	**16.**	50
17.	11	**18.**	3
19.	6	**20.**	27
21.	20	**22.**	56
23.	99	**24.**	6
25.	34	**26.**	55
27.	45	**28.**	49
29.	16	**30.**	3
31.	9	**32.**	240
33.	250	**34.**	36
35.	12	**36.**	7
37.	60	**38.**	48
39.	63	**40.**	5

Page 56
1.	18	**2.**	90
3.	36	**4.**	60
5.	30	**6.**	40
7.	4	**8.**	11
9.	24	**10.**	8
11.	5	**12.**	48
13.	9	**14.**	1.2
15.	100	**16.**	7
17.	32	**18.**	40
19.	8	**20.**	40

Answers

21.	48	**22.**	850
23.	60	**24.**	7
25.	16	**26.**	22
27.	60	**28.**	350
29.	15	**30.**	9
31.	6	**32.**	121
33.	5	**34.**	54
35.	4	**36.**	2
37.	32	**38.**	7
39.	14	**40.**	144

Published by Letts Educational
An imprint of HarperCollins*Publishers* Ltd
1 London Bridge Street
London SE1 9GF

ISBN 9781844198627

Text © 2015 Paul Broadbent

Design © 2015 Letts Educational, an imprint of
HarperCollins*Publishers* Ltd

Fractions of amounts

2. Complete by writing < or > between each pair of amounts.

a) $\frac{2}{3}$ of 90 ☐ $\frac{7}{10}$ of 90   **b)** $\frac{3}{4}$ of 100 ☐ $\frac{4}{5}$ of 100

c) $\frac{3}{10}$ of 140 ☐ $\frac{2}{7}$ of 140   **d)** $\frac{5}{8}$ of 160 ☐ $\frac{3}{4}$ of 160

3. Answer these.

a) What fraction of £1 is:	**b) What fraction of £2 is:**	**c) What fraction of £10 is:**
50p ⟶ ____	20p ⟶ ____	£2.50 ⟶ ____
20p ⟶ ____	£1 ⟶ ____	£5 ⟶ ____
10p ⟶ ____	50p ⟶ ____	£1 ⟶ ____
25p ⟶ ____	£1.50 ⟶ ____	£7.50 ⟶ ____
75p ⟶ ____	40p ⟶ ____	£2 ⟶ ____

4. Read and answer these.

a) Would it be lighter to carry $\frac{1}{5}$ of 10 kg or $\frac{1}{10}$ of 10 kg?

_____

b) Joy wants a large slice of cake. Should she cut the cake into quarters or thirds to get the largest slice?

_____

c) There are 24 hours in a day. Peter spends a quarter of the day at school and a third asleep. Does he spend more time at school or more time sleeping?

_____

d) There are 45 fish. $\frac{3}{5}$ are spotted and $\frac{2}{9}$ are striped. Are there more striped or more spotted fish?

_____

Fraction calculations

Remember that to add and subtract fractions with the same denominator, just add or subtract the numerators.

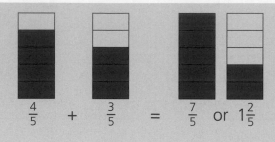

$$\frac{4}{5} \quad + \quad \frac{3}{5} \quad = \quad \frac{7}{5} \quad \text{or} \quad 1\frac{2}{5}$$

$$1\frac{2}{5} - \frac{3}{5} = \underline{\quad\quad}$$

If it is a mixed number, change it to an improper fraction.

$$\frac{7}{5} - \frac{3}{5} = \frac{4}{5}$$

Practice activities

1. Join pairs of fractions that total 3.

$1\frac{3}{4}$ $\qquad\qquad$ $1\frac{7}{8}$ $\qquad\qquad$ $1\frac{1}{8}$

$\qquad\quad$ $\frac{2}{3}$ $\qquad\qquad\qquad$ $\frac{7}{10}$

$2\frac{3}{10}$ $\qquad\qquad$ $1\frac{1}{3}$ $\qquad\qquad$ $1\frac{2}{3}$

$\qquad$ $2\frac{1}{3}$ $\qquad\qquad$ $1\frac{1}{4}$

2. Subtract these fractions.

a) $\frac{9}{4} - \frac{1}{4} = \underline{\quad\quad}$ $\qquad\qquad$ b) $\frac{7}{10} - \frac{1}{10} = \underline{\quad\quad}$

c) $\frac{12}{5} - \frac{3}{5} = \underline{\quad\quad}$ $\qquad\qquad$ d) $\frac{11}{10} - \frac{3}{10} = \underline{\quad\quad}$

3. Add the shaded parts of these shapes.

a)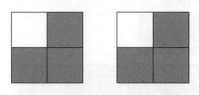

$\frac{3}{4} + \frac{3}{4} =$ _____ or _____

b)

$\frac{5}{6} + \frac{2}{6} =$ _____ or _____

c)

$\frac{3}{10} + \frac{8}{10} =$ _____ or _____

d)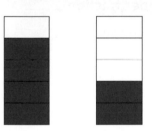

$\frac{4}{5} + \frac{2}{5} =$ _____ or _____

4. Subtract these fractions. Change mixed numbers to improper fractions to make them easier.

a) $1\frac{1}{4} - \frac{3}{4} =$ _____

b) $1\frac{2}{5} - \frac{4}{5} =$ _____

c) $1\frac{3}{10} - \frac{6}{10} =$ _____

d) $1\frac{1}{3} - \frac{2}{3} =$ _____

5. Answer these. Give your answers as fractions or mixed numbers as appropriate.

a) Add together $\frac{1}{4}$ and $6\frac{3}{4}$. _____

b) What is the difference between $1\frac{3}{10}$ m and $\frac{7}{10}$ m? _____ m

c) Total $4\frac{3}{5}$ and $1\frac{3}{5}$. _____

d) How much more is $3\frac{1}{10}$ litres than $\frac{8}{10}$ litres? _____ litres

e) What is the sum of $1\frac{3}{4}$ and $6\frac{3}{4}$? _____

Mental arithmetic test 7

1. $\frac{1}{6}$ of 24 = _____

2. What fraction of £5 is £1.25?

   _____

3. Circle **two** fractions that total 5.

   $1\frac{1}{2}$ $2\frac{1}{2}$

          $4\frac{1}{2}$ $3\frac{1}{2}$

4. Write this as:

   an **improper fraction** _____

   a **mixed number** _____

5. $\frac{14}{4} - \frac{3}{4}$ = _____

6. Write $2\frac{7}{10}$ as an improper fraction.

   _____

7. Circle the smallest fraction and underline the greatest fraction.

   $\frac{7}{3}$ $1\frac{2}{3}$ $\frac{8}{3}$ $1\frac{1}{3}$ $\frac{6}{3}$

8. Add together $\frac{1}{3}$ and $4\frac{2}{3}$.

   _____

9. Write these fractions in order.

   $\frac{1}{10}$ $\frac{1}{2}$ $\frac{1}{7}$ $\frac{1}{4}$

   _____ < _____ < _____ < _____

10. Circle **two** of these with the same value.

    $1\frac{4}{5}$ $3\frac{1}{5}$ $\frac{13}{5}$

          $\frac{9}{5}$ $\frac{14}{5}$ $1\frac{3}{5}$

11. Add these and write the answer as an **improper fraction** and a **mixed number**.

    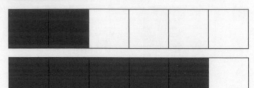

    $\frac{2}{6} + \frac{5}{6}$ = _____ or _____

12. $\frac{1}{8}$ of 72 = _____

13. $1\frac{2}{9} - \frac{4}{9}$ = _____

14. How much is $\frac{1}{5}$ of £1? _____

15. Write the fraction at the arrow as:

    an **improper fraction** _____

    a **mixed number** _____

    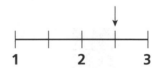

16. Write the answer as an improper fraction and a mixed number.

    $\frac{8}{9} + \frac{6}{9}$ = _____ or _____

17. In a bag of 30 balloons, $\frac{3}{10}$ are pink and $\frac{2}{5}$ are blue. Which are there more of, pink or blue balloons?

    _____

18. Write $\frac{5}{3}$ as a mixed number. _____

19. $\frac{7}{10}$ of 120 = _____

20. Write < or > to make this true.

    $\frac{7}{10}$ of 40 _____ $\frac{4}{5}$ of 40

Score   /20

34

1. Write this as:

an **improper fraction** _____

a **mixed number** _____

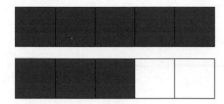

2. $\frac{1}{6}$ of 30 = _____

3. Add together $\frac{1}{2}$ and $7\frac{1}{2}$. _____

4. How much is $\frac{1}{4}$ of £2? _____

5. Write $\frac{7}{2}$ as a mixed number. _____

6. In a box of 21 fruits, $\frac{3}{7}$ are apples and $\frac{1}{3}$ are oranges. Which are there more of, apples or oranges?

_____

7. Write < or > to make this true.

$\frac{3}{4}$ of 60 _____ $\frac{4}{5}$ of 60

8. $\frac{12}{8} - \frac{7}{8} =$ _____

9. Circle **two** of these with the same value.

$2\frac{1}{3}$ $\frac{3}{3}$ $1\frac{2}{3}$

$\frac{5}{3}$ $2\frac{2}{3}$ $\frac{4}{3}$

10. Add these and write the answer as an **improper fraction** and a **mixed number**.

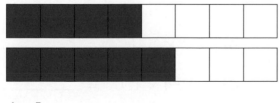

$\frac{4}{8} + \frac{5}{8} =$ _____ or _____

11. Circle the smallest fraction and underline the greatest fraction.

$2\frac{1}{5}$ $\frac{12}{5}$ $2\frac{3}{5}$ $\frac{8}{5}$ $1\frac{4}{5}$

12. $1\frac{2}{7} - \frac{5}{7} =$ _____

13. $\frac{3}{10}$ of 150 = _____

14. Circle **two** fractions that total 4.

$3\frac{1}{4}$ $\frac{1}{4}$ $2\frac{3}{4}$

$1\frac{3}{4}$ $2\frac{1}{4}$

15. What fraction of £5 is 50p? _____

16. Write $1\frac{3}{10}$ as an improper fraction. _____

17. Write these fractions in order.

$\frac{1}{6}$ $\frac{1}{5}$ $\frac{1}{8}$ $\frac{1}{3}$

_____ < _____ < _____ < _____

18. Write the answer as an improper fraction and a mixed number.

$\frac{5}{9} + \frac{6}{9} =$ _____ or _____

19. Write the fraction at the arrow as:

an **improper fraction** _____

a **mixed number** _____

20. $\frac{5}{9}$ of 63 = _____

Score   /20

Decimals

Learn and revise

Follow these rules for multiplying and dividing numbers by 10 and 100.

To multiply by 10

Move the digits one place to the left.

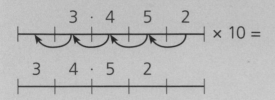

To multiply by 100

Move the digits two places to the left.

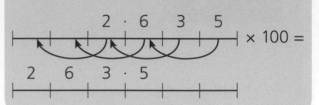

To divide by 10

Move the digits one place to the right.

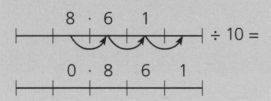

To divide by 100

Move the digits two places to the right.

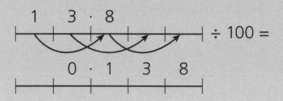

Practice activities

1. Multiply these by 10 and write the answers.

a) 0.34 × 10 = _____   b) 8.6 × 10   = _____

c) 1.228 × 10 = _____   d) 0.855 × 10 = _____

e) 3.72 × 10 = _____   f) 1.62 × 10   = _____

2. Multiply these by 100 and write the answers.

a) 3.68 × 100 = _____   b) 0.3 × 100   = _____

c) 1.005 × 100 = _____   d) 2.934 × 100 = _____

e) 0.655 × 100 = _____   f) 46.385 × 100 = _____

3. Divide these by 10 and write the answers.

a) 83.5 ÷ 10 = _____

b) 19 ÷ 10 = _____

c) 227.6 ÷ 10 = _____

d) 28.45 ÷ 10 = _____

e) 0.93 ÷ 10 = _____

f) 12.84 ÷ 10 = _____

4. Divide these by 100 and write the answers.

a) 27 ÷ 100 = _____

b) 342 ÷ 100 = _____

c) 53.8 ÷ 100 = _____

d) 6.3 ÷ 100 = _____

e) 27.9 ÷ 100 = _____

f) 145.2 ÷ 100 = _____

5. Write these weights in order starting with the lightest.

| 8.245 kg | 0.95 kg | 8.3 kg | 0.855 kg |

| 8.455 kg | | 8.52 kg | |

_____

6. Round each decimal number to the nearest tenth. Use the number line to help you.

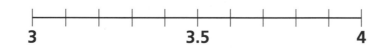

a) 3.25 _____

b) 3.83 _____

c) 3.08 _____

d) 3.574 _____

e) 3.908 _____

f) 3.445 _____

Fractions, decimals and percentages

Practice activities

1. Write each of these fractions as a percentage.

   a) $\frac{1}{2}$ = ____%

   b) $\frac{1}{4}$ = ____%

   c) $\frac{1}{10}$ = ____%

   d) $\frac{1}{5}$ = ____%

   e) $\frac{3}{5}$ = ____%

   f) $\frac{18}{25}$ = ____%

   g) $\frac{29}{50}$ = ____%

   h) $\frac{13}{20}$ = ____%

   i) $\frac{4}{5}$ = ____%

   j) $\frac{3}{10}$ = ____%

   k) $\frac{17}{50}$ = ____%

   l) $\frac{11}{20}$ = ____%

2. Write each of these percentages as a fraction reduced to its simplest form.

   a) 10% = ____

   b) 80% = ____

   c) 50% = ____

   d) 30% = ____

   e) 60% = ____

   f) 25% = ____

   g) 5% = ____

   h) 90% = ____

   i) 75% = ____

   j) 40% = ____

   k) 70% = ____

   l) 1% = ____

Fractions, decimals and percentages

3. Write each of these decimals as a percentage.

a) 0.2 = ____%

b) 0.15 = ____%

c) 0.35 = ____%

d) 0.6 = ____%

e) 0.5 = ____%

f) 0.3 = ____%

g) 0.75 = ____%

h) 0.9 = ____%

i) 0.85 = ____%

j) 0.1 = ____%

k) 0.05 = ____%

l) 0.7 = ____%

4. Write each of these percentages as a decimal.

a) 30% = _____

b) 45% = _____

c) 65% = _____

d) 80% = _____

e) 90% = _____

f) 25% = _____

g) 5% = _____

h) 15% = _____

i) 30% = _____

j) 55% = _____

k) 35% = _____

l) 85% = _____

5. Order these fractions and percentages from smallest to largest.
You may find it helpful to change all the fractions to percentages.

a)

$\frac{4}{5}$	15%	25%	$\frac{9}{25}$	20%	$\frac{6}{10}$

____ ____ ____ ____ ____ ____

smallest

b)

40%	$\frac{23}{50}$	$\frac{1}{4}$	10%	$\frac{7}{10}$	60%

____ ____ ____ ____ ____ ____

smallest

c)

3%	$\frac{3}{20}$	50%	$\frac{1}{10}$	16%	$\frac{1}{50}$

____ ____ ____ ____ ____ ____

smallest

Decimal calculations

Learn and revise

Use facts you know to calculate with decimals. Look at the numbers and decide on the best strategy to work out the answer.

Use near doubles.

Example: What is 3.6 + 3.5?

$$3.5 + 3.5 = 7$$

So 3.5 + 3.6 = 7.1

Count on or back in different jumps.

Example: What is 9.2 − 6.8?

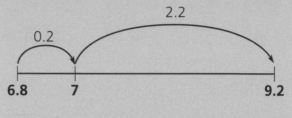

9.2 − 6.8 = 2.4

Partition, or break numbers up.

Example: What is 4.8 × 5?

$$4 \times 5 = 20$$

$$0.8 \times 5 = 4$$

So 4.8 × 5 = 24

Use facts you know.

Example: What is 0.9 × 7?

$$9 \times 7 = 63$$

So 0.9 × 7 = 6.3

Practice activities

1. Join each of these to the matching answer.

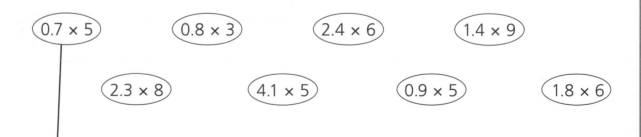

| 0.7 × 5 | 0.8 × 3 | 2.4 × 6 | 1.4 × 9 |

| 2.3 × 8 | 4.1 × 5 | 0.9 × 5 | 1.8 × 6 |

| **3.5** | **2.4** | **12.6** | **10.8** | **14.4** | **18.4** | **4.5** | **20.5** |

Decimal calculations

2. Answer these.

    a) 0.6 + 3.9 = _____   **b)** 2.8 + 0.8 = _____   **c)** 4.7 + 0.9 = _____

    d) 6.8 + 2.4 = _____   **e)** 5.4 + 1.7 = _____   **f)** 7.5 + 2.8 = _____

3. Use the number lines to help answer these subtractions.

    a) 7.8 – 3.4 = _____

    b) 2.5 – 1.7 = _____

    c) 8.9 – 3.5 = _____

    d) 4.2 – 2.8 = _____

    e) 9.4 – 6.9 = _____

    f) 7.4 – 2.6 = _____

4. Write the missing digits, 0–5, in these calculations.

| 0 | 1 | 2 | 3 | 4 | 5 |

$\boxed{}.\boxed{} \times \boxed{6} = \boxed{1}.\boxed{8}$ $\boxed{3}.\boxed{4} \times \boxed{7} = \boxed{}\boxed{3}.\boxed{8}$

$\boxed{}.\boxed{9} \times \boxed{5} = \boxed{9}.\boxed{}$ $\boxed{2}.\boxed{6} \times \boxed{4} = \boxed{1}\boxed{0}.\boxed{}$

Mental arithmetic test 9

1. $\frac{1}{2}$ = _____%

2. 6.8 × 2 = _____

3. 5.432 × 10 = _____

4. Circle the smallest and underline the largest fraction or percentage in this set.

   $\frac{13}{50}$ 25% $\frac{7}{25}$ 24% $\frac{1}{4}$ 27%

5. Write 30% as a fraction, in its simplest form.

   _____

6. Write the missing digits.

   80% = 0._____ = $\frac{\square}{5}$

7. Write < or > to make this true.

   4.119 km _____ 4.19 km

8. 73 ÷ 100 = _____

9. 3.2 × 4 = _____

10. Circle the heaviest weight and underline the lightest weight.

    5.2 kg   5.29 kg   2.995 kg

    5.02 kg   0.925 kg

11. Write < or > to make this true.

    30% _____ 0.03

12. 0.9 = _____%

13. 0.87 × 100 = _____

14. Round each decimal to the nearest tenth.

    4.17 $\longrightarrow$ _____

    4.017 $\longrightarrow$ _____

15. 4 × 0.7 = _____

16. 12 ÷ 100 = _____

17. Write 65% as a decimal.

    _____

18. 61.9 ÷ 10 = _____

19. Round these to the nearest tenth.

    1.508 $\longrightarrow$ _____

    1.58 $\longrightarrow$ _____

20. Use this number line to help you work out this subtraction.

    |————————————————|
    1.7   2.2

    2.2 − 1.7 = _____

Score   /20

Mental arithmetic test 10

1. Write 75% as a fraction, in its simplest form.

   _____

2. $19.6 \div 10 =$ _____

3. $7.004 \times 100 =$ _____

4. $0.8 \times 6 =$ _____

5. Round these to the nearest tenth.

   $2.83 \longrightarrow$ _____

   $2.083 \longrightarrow$ _____

6. Use this number line to help you work out this subtraction.

   ├─────────────────────┤
   1.8   3.7

   $3.7 - 1.8 =$ _____

7. $0.57 \times 10 =$ _____

8. $3.6 + 0.9 =$ _____

9. $0.45 =$ _____%

10. Write < or > to make this true.

    70% _____ $\frac{3}{5}$

11. Circle the smallest and underline the largest fraction or percentage in this set.

    $\frac{8}{25}$ 25% $\frac{7}{20}$ 30% $\frac{3}{10}$

12. $1.9 \times 2 =$ _____

13. $\frac{1}{4} =$ _____%

14. $8.24 \times 100 =$ _____

15. $109.3 \div 100 =$ _____

16. Write < or > to make this true.

    $6.75\,km$ _____ $6.507\,km$

17. $1.3 + 9.8 =$ _____

18. Circle the heaviest weight and underline the lightest weight.

    2.03 kg   2.305 kg   3.05 kg

    2.3 kg   0.532 kg

19. $34 \div 100 =$ _____

20. Write 70% as a decimal.

    _____

Score   /20

43

Square numbers

Learn and revise

Look at this pattern.

1   4   9   16

The numbers 1, 4, 9 and 16 are examples of **square numbers**, when two identical whole numbers are multiplied together.

1 squared is written as 1^2.

$1^2 \longrightarrow 1 \times 1 = 1$

$2^2 \longrightarrow 2 \times 2 = 4$

$3^2 \longrightarrow 3 \times 3 = 9$

$4^2 \longrightarrow 4 \times 4 = 16$

Practice activities

1. Answer these to find more square numbers.

   a) $8^2 =$ _____   b) $11^2 =$ _____

   c) $7^2 =$ _____   d) $6^2 =$ _____

   e) $9^2 =$ _____   f) $10^2 =$ _____

   g) $5^2 =$ _____   h) $12^2 =$ _____

2. Colour the square numbers on the grid on page 45. What do you notice?

   _____

×	1	2	3	4	5	6	7	8	9	10	11	12
1	1	2	3	4	5	6	7	8	9	10	11	12
2	2	4	6	8	10	12	14	16	18	20	22	24
3	3	6	9	12	15	18	21	24	27	30	33	36
4	4	8	12	16	20	24	28	32	36	40	44	48
5	5	10	15	20	25	30	35	40	45	50	55	60
6	6	12	18	24	30	36	42	48	54	60	66	72
7	7	14	21	28	35	42	49	56	63	70	77	84
8	8	16	24	32	40	48	56	64	72	80	88	96
9	9	18	27	36	45	54	63	72	81	90	99	108
10	10	20	30	40	50	60	70	80	90	100	110	120
11	11	22	33	44	55	66	77	88	99	110	121	132
12	12	24	36	48	60	72	84	96	108	120	132	144

3. Add these consecutive odd numbers and write the total.

a) 1 + 3   = ____

b) 1 + 3 + 5   = ____

c) 1 + 3 + 5 + 7   = ____

d) 1 + 3 + 5 + 7 + 9   = ____

e) 1 + 3 + 5 + 7 + 9 + 11   = ____

f) 1 + 3 + 5 + 7 + 9 + 11 + 13   = ____

g) 1 + 3 + 5 + 7 + 9 + 11 + 13 + 15   = ____

h) 1 + 3 + 5 + 7 + 9 + 11 + 13 + 15 + 17   = ____

i) 1 + 3 + 5 + 7 + 9 + 11 + 13 + 15 + 17 + 19 = ____

4. Look at the answers in practice activity 3. What do you notice about them?

_____

Area and perimeter

The area of this rectangle is 30 square centimetres or 30 cm². It can be calculated by multiplying the length by the width.

6 cm

5 cm

Area = 6 cm × 5 cm = 30 cm²

Area of rectangle = Length × Width $A = L \times W$

The perimeter is the distance all the way around a shape. Add together the length of each side of the rectangle.

6 cm + 6 cm + 5 cm + 5 cm = 22 cm

Perimeter = 22 cm

Perimeter of rectangle = 2 × (Length + Width) $P = 2 \times (L + W)$

Practice activities

1. What are the area and perimeter of each of these?

a)

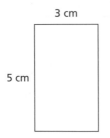

3 cm

5 cm

Area = _____ cm²

Perimeter = _____ cm

b)

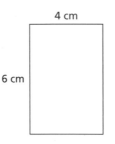

4 cm

6 cm

Area = _____ cm²

Perimeter = _____ cm

c)

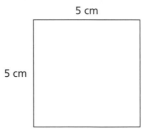

5 cm

5 cm

Area = _____ cm²

Perimeter = _____ cm

d)

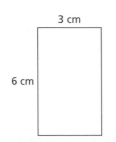

3 cm

6 cm

Area = _____ cm²

Perimeter = _____ cm

e)

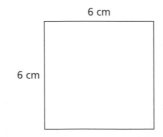

6 cm

6 cm

Area = _____ cm²

Perimeter = _____ cm

f)

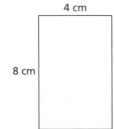

4 cm

8 cm

Area = _____ cm²

Perimeter = _____ cm

Area and perimeter

2. This table shows the length and width of different rectangles.
   Complete the table.

Length (L)	Width (W)	Area (cm²) $L \times W$	Perimeter (cm) $2 \times (L + W)$
12 cm	3 cm		
4 cm	10 cm		
6 cm	8 cm		
7 cm	7 cm		
5 cm	8 cm		
15 cm	3 cm		
4 cm	13 cm		
20 cm	5 cm		
18 cm	3 cm		
11 cm	11 cm		
16 cm	4 cm		
20 cm	20 cm		

3. The area of a square is 16 cm².

   a) What is the length of each side? _____ cm

   b) What is the perimeter of the square? _____ cm

4. The perimeter of a square is 36 cm.

   a) What is the length of each side? _____ cm

   b) What is the area of the square? _____ cm²

Time

Learn and revise

The duration of an event is how much time it takes. A timeline is very useful to help work this out.

Example:

A film starts at 6.40 p.m. and finishes at 8.15 p.m. How long does the film last?

Use a timeline and count on from the start to the finish:

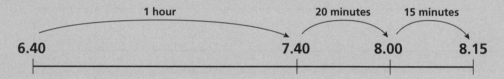

1 hour + 20 minutes + 15 minutes is 1 hour 35 minutes.

So the film lasts for 1 hour 35 minutes.

Practice activities

1. Write the time that is:

   a) 40 minutes later than 5.25 p.m. _____

   b) 25 minutes later than 8.50 a.m. _____

   c) 20 minutes earlier than 10.50 a.m. _____

   d) 45 minutes earlier than 4.20 p.m. _____

   e) 1 hour 10 minutes later than 7.45 p.m. _____

2. Answer these.

a) It takes Ben 35 minutes to walk to school.

If he arrives at 8.50 a.m., at what time does he leave home? _____

b) Jim drove a lorry from 6.55 a.m. until 8.40 a.m. before taking a rest.

How long had he been driving for? _____

c) A market stall opens at 8.15 a.m. and closes at 1.05 p.m.

How long is the stall open for? _____

d) David ran a half-marathon and finished in 1 hour 35 minutes.

If the race started at 10.15 a.m., what time did he finish? _____

e) Alice falls asleep at 8.50 p.m. and sleeps for 9 hours 25 minutes.

What time does she wake up? _____

3. Look at this bus timetable.

	Bus A	Bus B	Bus C	Bus D
School	8.15 a.m.	9.35 a.m.	11.05 a.m.	1.55 p.m.
Hospital	8.35 a.m.	9.50 a.m.	11.30 a.m.	2.15 p.m.
Market	8.45 a.m.	10.00 a.m.	11.40 a.m.	2.35 p.m.
Town Centre	9.10 a.m.	10.30 a.m.	12.05 p.m.	2.45 p.m.

a) Which is the fastest bus from the school to the town centre?

_____

b) Which is the slowest bus from the hospital to the town centre?

_____

Mental arithmetic test 11

1. $4^2 =$ _____

2. What is the area of a room in the shape of a rectangle with sides 3 m wide and 4 m long?

   _____ m²

3. What time is 45 minutes later than 3.20 p.m.?

   _____

4.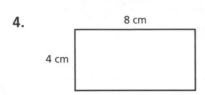

   Area   = _____ cm²

   Perimeter = _____ cm

5. A film starts at 7.15 p.m. and finishes at 8.40 p.m. How long is the film?

   _____

6. The perimeter of a square is 28 cm. What is the length of each side?

   _____ cm

7. Shobna's dance class starts at 10.10 a.m. and lasts for 1 hour 30 minutes. What time does the dance class finish?

   _____

8. $9^2 =$ _____

9. What is the perimeter of a photo frame in the shape of a rectangle with sides 15 cm wide and 25 cm long?

   _____ cm

10. The area of a square is 100 cm². What is the length of each side?

    _____ cm

11. Circle the square number.

    48   55

         36   60

12. How long is 55 minutes and 45 minutes in total?

    _____

13.

    9 cm

    3 cm

    Area   = _____ cm²

    Perimeter = _____ cm

14. A bus leaves at 5.30 p.m., drives 15 minutes to the doctor's and drives another 25 minutes to the bus station. What time does it arrive at the bus station?

    _____

15. $12^2 =$ _____

16. The area of a square is 64 cm². What is the length of each side?

    _____ cm

17. What is the next square number?

    4   9   16   _____

    These are the times of a TV show Maths Fun! Use this information in 18–20.

Maths Fun!	Saturday	Sunday
Starts	11.40 a.m.	4.55 p.m.
Finishes	12.25 p.m.	6.10 p.m.

18. On which day is Maths Fun! on TV in the morning?

    _____

19. How long is the Saturday Maths Fun! show?

    _____

20. Which is the longest Maths Fun! show, Saturday or Sunday?

    _____

Score   /20

1.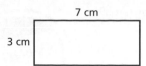

   7 cm

   3 cm

   Area = _____ cm²

   Perimeter = _____ cm

2. 7^2 = _____

3. A shop closes at 12.30 p.m. for 45 minutes for lunch. What time does the shop re-open after lunch?

   _____

4. The perimeter of a square is 12 cm. What is the length of each side?

   _____ cm

5. What time is 20 minutes before 7.15 p.m.?

   _____

6. 8^2 = _____

7. What is the area of a garden in the shape of a rectangle 6 m wide and 9 m long?

   _____ m²

Use these swimming times in 8–10.

Swim Class	Saturday	Sunday
Starts	10.35 a.m.	11.20 a.m.
Finishes	11.50 a.m.	12.45 p.m.

8. Jo wants a class that starts as late as possible. Which class is at the later time, Saturday or Sunday?

   _____

9. How long is Sunday's class?

   _____

10. Which is the shorter swimming class, Saturday or Sunday?

   _____

11. What is the perimeter of a pond in the shape of a rectangle 2 m wide and 3 m long?

   _____ m

12. I wake at 7.30 a.m. I take 15 minutes to dress and 10 minutes to eat breakfast, then I am ready. At what time am I ready?

   _____

13. What time is 1 hour 30 minutes later than 4.50 p.m.?

   _____

14. The area of a square is 81 cm². What is the length of each side?

   _____ cm

15. 11^2 = _____

16. Class B's Maths lesson starts at 9.55 a.m. and ends at 10.40 a.m. How long is Class B's Maths lesson?

   _____ minutes

17. What is the next square number?

   1   4   9   _____

18.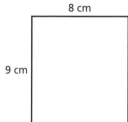

   8 cm

   9 cm

   Area = _____ cm²

   Perimeter = _____ cm

19. How long is 1 hour 20 minutes and 50 minutes altogether?

   _____

20. Circle the square number.

   30   44

   18   25

Score   /20

51

Speed test

- How many of these can you complete correctly in one minute?
- Write your answers on paper. Number them 1 to 40.
- Don't worry if you cannot answer them all, just answer them as quickly as you can.
- Stop after one minute, check your answers and record your score on the progress chart opposite.
- Then, try again at another time to see if you can improve your score!

Addition and subtraction

1. $20 + 70$ = _____	**21.** $20 + 90$ = _____
2. $9 + 8$ = _____	**22.** $60 + 40$ = _____
3. $13 + 7$ = _____	**23.** $19 - 6$ = _____
4. $16 - 9$ = _____	**24.** $11 - 7$ = _____
5. $20 - 13$ = _____	**25.** $6 + 7$ = _____
6. $15 + 6$ = _____	**26.** $110 - 90$ = _____
7. $80 - 30$ = _____	**27.** $0.8 - 0.3$ = _____
8. $9 + 7$ = _____	**28.** $16 - 12$ = _____
9. $100 - 50$ = _____	**29.** $13 - 4$ = _____
10. $800 - 600$ = _____	**30.** $17 - 11$ = _____
11. $120 - 30$ = _____	**31.** $50 + 40$ = _____
12. $15 + 8$ = _____	**32.** $17 + 8$ = _____
13. $150 + 150$ = _____	**33.** $\frac{4}{5} - \frac{1}{5}$ = _____
14. $\frac{2}{5} + \frac{2}{5}$ = _____	**34.** $9 + 6$ = _____
15. $70 + 70$ = _____	**35.** $13 - 8$ = _____
16. $21 - 3$ = _____	**36.** $80 + 50$ = _____
17. $400 + 500$ = _____	**37.** $18 + 4$ = _____
18. $0.5 + 0.3$ = _____	**38.** $27 - 5$ = _____
19. $12 - 9$ = _____	**39.** $16 + 6$ = _____
20. $7 + 8$ = _____	**40.** $100 - 40$ = _____

Progress chart

Colour in the stars to show your correct answers.

	Attempt	1	2	3	4	5	6
	Date						

Scores out of 40

Attempt 1: 39 40 / 37 38 / 35 36 / 33 34 / 31 32 / 29 30 / 27 28 / 25 26 / 23 24 / 21 22 / 19 20 / 17 18 / 15 16 / 13 14 / 11 12 / 9 10 / 7 8 / 5 6 / 3 4 / 1 2

Attempt 2: 39 40 / 37 38 / 35 36 / 33 34 / 31 32 / 29 30 / 27 28 / 25 26 / 23 24 / 21 22 / 19 20 / 17 18 / 15 16 / 13 14 / 11 12 / 9 10 / 7 8 / 5 6 / 3 4 / 1 2

Attempt 3: 39 40 / 37 38 / 35 36 / 33 34 / 31 32 / 29 30 / 27 28 / 25 26 / 23 24 / 21 22 / 19 20 / 17 18 / 15 16 / 13 14 / 11 12 / 9 10 / 7 8 / 5 6 / 3 4 / 1 2

Attempt 4: 39 40 / 37 38 / 35 36 / 33 34 / 31 32 / 29 30 / 27 28 / 25 26 / 23 24 / 21 22 / 19 20 / 17 18 / 15 16 / 13 14 / 11 12 / 9 10 / 7 8 / 5 6 / 3 4 / 1 2

Attempt 5: 39 40 / 37 38 / 35 36 / 33 34 / 31 32 / 29 30 / 27 28 / 25 26 / 23 24 / 21 22 / 19 20 / 17 18 / 15 16 / 13 14 / 11 12 / 9 10 / 7 8 / 5 6 / 3 4 / 1 2

Attempt 6: 39 40 / 37 38 / 35 36 / 33 34 / 31 32 / 29 30 / 27 28 / 25 26 / 23 24 / 21 22 / 19 20 / 17 18 / 15 16 / 13 14 / 11 12 / 9 10 / 7 8 / 5 6 / 3 4 / 1 2

Speed test

- How many of these can you complete correctly in one minute?
- Write your answers on paper. Number them 1 to 40.
- Don't worry if you cannot answer them all, just answer them as quickly as you can.
- Stop after one minute, check your answers and record your score on the progress chart opposite.
- Then, try again at another time to see if you can improve your score!

Multiplication and division

1. 6 × 5 = _____
2. 8 × 4 = _____
3. 55 ÷ 11 = _____
4. 16 ÷ 8 = _____
5. 6 × 3 = _____
6. 12 × 5 = _____
7. 30 ÷ 6 = _____
8. 15 ÷ 3 = _____
9. 9 × 2 = _____
10. 90 ÷ 9 = _____
11. 80 ÷ 4 = _____
12. 4 × 6 = _____
13. 12 × 10 = _____
14. 32 ÷ 8 = _____
15. 6 × 7 = _____
16. 5 × 10 = _____
17. 110 ÷ 10 = _____
18. 21 ÷ 7 = _____
19. 36 ÷ 6 = _____
20. 3 × 9 = _____

21. 40 ÷ 2 = _____
22. 8 × 7 = _____
23. 9 × 11 = _____
24. 18 ÷ 3 = _____
25. 3.4 × 10 = _____
26. 11 × 5 = _____
27. 5 × 9 = _____
28. 7 × 7 = _____
29. 160 ÷ 10 = _____
30. 24 ÷ 8 = _____
31. 54 ÷ 6 = _____
32. 40 × 6 = _____
33. 25 × 10 = _____
34. 6 × 6 = _____
35. 120 ÷ 10 = _____
36. 28 ÷ 4 = _____
37. 2 × 30 = _____
38. 8 × 6 = _____
39. 9 × 7 = _____
40. 25 ÷ 5 = _____

Progress chart

Colour in the stars to show your correct answers.

Attempt	1	2	3	4	5	6
Date	....	....	....	....	....	....

Scores out of 40

	1		2		3		4		5		6	
	39	40	39	40	39	40	39	40	39	40	39	40
	37	38	37	38	37	38	37	38	37	38	37	38
	35	36	35	36	35	36	35	36	35	36	35	36
	33	34	33	34	33	34	33	34	33	34	33	34
	31	32	31	32	31	32	31	32	31	32	31	32
	29	30	29	30	29	30	29	30	29	30	29	30
	27	28	27	28	27	28	27	28	27	28	27	28
	25	26	25	26	25	26	25	26	25	26	25	26
	23	24	23	24	23	24	23	24	23	24	23	24
	21	22	21	22	21	22	21	22	21	22	21	22
	19	20	19	20	19	20	19	20	19	20	19	20
	17	18	17	18	17	18	17	18	17	18	17	18
	15	16	15	16	15	16	15	16	15	16	15	16
	13	14	13	14	13	14	13	14	13	14	13	14
	11	12	11	12	11	12	11	12	11	12	11	12
	9	10	9	10	9	10	9	10	9	10	9	10
	7	8	7	8	7	8	7	8	7	8	7	8
	5	6	5	6	5	6	5	6	5	6	5	6
	3	4	3	4	3	4	3	4	3	4	3	4
	1	2	1	2	1	2	1	2	1	2	1	2

Speed test

- How many of these can you complete correctly in one minute?
- Write your answers on paper. Number them 1 to 40.
- Don't worry if you cannot answer them all, just answer them as quickly as you can.
- Stop after one minute, check your answers and record your score on the progress chart opposite.
- Then, try again at another time to see if you can improve your score!

Mixed problems

1. 9 + 9 = _____

2. 30 + 60 = _____

3. 9 × 4 = _____

4. 90 – 30 = _____

5. 60 ÷ 2 = _____

6. 90 – 50 = _____

7. 36 ÷ 9 = _____

8. 7 + 4 = _____

9. 3 × 8 = _____

10. 88 ÷ 11 = _____

11. 12 – 7 = _____

12. 12 × 4 = _____

13. 15 – 6 = _____

14. 0.6 + 0.6 = _____

15. 50 + 50 = _____

16. 35 ÷ 5 = _____

17. 4 × 8 = _____

18. 70 – 30 = _____

19. 32 ÷ 4 = _____

20. 8 × 5 = _____

21. 6 × 8 = _____

22. 650 + 200 = _____

23. 180 ÷ 3 = _____

24. 12 – 5 = _____

25. 4 × 4 = _____

26. 19 + 3 = _____

27. 80 – 20 = _____

28. 70 × 5 = _____

29. 7 + 8 = _____

30. 18 – 9 = _____

31. 36 ÷ 6 = _____

32. 11 × 11 = _____

33. 13 – 8 = _____

34. 9 × 6 = _____

35. 28 ÷ 7 = _____

36. 12 ÷ 6 = _____

37. 8 × 4 = _____

38. 15 – 8 = _____

39. 9 + 5 = _____

40. 12 × 12 = _____

Progress chart

Colour in the stars to show your correct answers.

Attempt	1	2	3	4	5	6
Date	....	....	....	....	....	....
	39 40	39 40	39 40	39 40	39 40	39 40
	37 38	37 38	37 38	37 38	37 38	37 38
	35 36	35 36	35 36	35 36	35 36	35 36
	33 34	33 34	33 34	33 34	33 34	33 34
	31 32	31 32	31 32	31 32	31 32	31 32
	29 30	29 30	29 30	29 30	29 30	29 30
	27 28	27 28	27 28	27 28	27 28	27 28
	25 26	25 26	25 26	25 26	25 26	25 26
Scores out of 40	23 24	23 24	23 24	23 24	23 24	23 24
	21 22	21 22	21 22	21 22	21 22	21 22
	19 20	19 20	19 20	19 20	19 20	19 20
	17 18	17 18	17 18	17 18	17 18	17 18
	15 16	15 16	15 16	15 16	15 16	15 16
	13 14	13 14	13 14	13 14	13 14	13 14
	11 12	11 12	11 12	11 12	11 12	11 12
	9 10	9 10	9 10	9 10	9 10	9 10
	7 8	7 8	7 8	7 8	7 8	7 8
	5 6	5 6	5 6	5 6	5 6	5 6
	3 4	3 4	3 4	3 4	3 4	3 4
	1 2	1 2	1 2	1 2	1 2	1 2

Key facts

Multiplication and division facts

×	1	2	3	4	5	6	7	8	9	10	11	12
1	1	2	3	4	5	6	7	8	9	10	11	12
2	2	4	6	8	10	12	14	16	18	20	22	24
3	3	6	9	12	15	18	21	24	27	30	33	36
4	4	8	12	16	20	24	28	32	36	40	44	48
5	5	10	15	20	25	30	35	40	45	50	55	60
6	6	12	18	24	30	36	42	48	54	60	66	72
7	7	14	21	28	35	42	49	56	63	70	77	84
8	8	16	24	32	40	48	56	64	72	80	88	96
9	9	18	27	36	45	54	63	72	81	90	99	108
10	10	20	30	40	50	60	70	80	90	100	110	120
11	11	22	33	44	55	66	77	88	99	110	121	132
12	12	24	36	48	60	72	84	96	108	120	132	144

Fractions, decimals and percentages

$\frac{1}{2} = 0.5 = 50\%$	$\frac{1}{4} = 0.25 = 25\%$	$\frac{3}{4} = 0.75 = 75\%$
$\frac{1}{5} = 0.2 = 20\%$	$\frac{1}{10} = 0.1 = 10\%$	$\frac{2}{5} = 0.4 = 40\%$

A fraction has two parts:

$\frac{2}{3}$ ⟵ **numerator**
⟵ **denominator**

A **proper fraction** is less than 1.	An **improper fraction** is greater than 1.	A **mixed number** is made up of a whole number and a fraction.
The numerator is smaller than the denominator, e.g. $\frac{3}{5}$	The numerator is greater than the denominator, e.g. $\frac{5}{3}$	$\frac{5}{3} = 1\frac{2}{3}$

Multiples

A multiple of a whole number is produced by multiplying that number by another whole number.

Multiples of 3 ⟶ 3　6　9　**12**　15　18...　60...　300...

Multiples of 4 ⟶ 4　8　**12**　16　20　24...　80...　400...

12 is a **common multiple** of both 3 and 4.

Factors

The factors of 8 are **1**, **2**, **4** and **8**.

The factors of 24 are **1**, **2**, 3, **4**, 6, **8**, 12 and 24.

The factors of 32 are **1**, **2**, **4**, **8**, 16 and 32.

The **common factors** of 8, 24 and 32 are 1, 2, 4 and 8.

Measures

Length	Capacity	Weight/Mass
1 kilometre (km) = 1000 metres (m)	1 litre (l) = 1000 millilitres (ml)	1 kilogram (kg) = 1000 grams (g)
1 metre (m) = 100 centimetres (cm)	1 litre (l) = 100 centilitres (cl)	
1 centimetre (cm) = 10 millimetres (mm)		

Time

1 minute = 60 seconds

1 hour = 60 minutes

1 day = 24 hours

1 week = 7 days

1 fortnight = 14 days

1 year = 12 months = 365 days

leap year = 366 days

Acknowledgements

The author and publisher are grateful to the copyright holders for permission to use quoted materials and images.

P16 ©Matthew Cole; P16 © Bernil; P17 ©Natali Snailcat; P28 ©Matthew Cole; P30 ©Matthew Cole; P30 ©Emeric; P31 ©Rinslet; P49 ©Paul Kooi; P52, 54, 56 ©Elmm The above images have been used under license from Shutterstock.com

All other images are © Letts Educational, an imprint of HarperCollins*Publishers* Ltd

Published by Letts Educational
An imprint of HarperCollins*Publishers* Ltd
1 London Bridge Street
London SE1 9GF

ISBN 9781844198627

First published 2013

This edition published 2015

10 9 8 7 6 5 4 3 2 1

Text © 2015 Paul Broadbent

Design © 2015 Letts Educational, an imprint of HarperCollins*Publishers* Ltd

British Library Cataloguing in Publication Data.

A CIP record of this book is available from the British Library.

Commissioning Editor: Tammy Poggo

Author: Paul Broadbent

Project Manager: Richard Toms

Editorial: Amanda Dickson, Richard Toms and Marie Taylor

Cover Design: Sarah Duxbury

Inside Concept Design: Ian Wrigley

Layout: Jouve India Private Limited

Printed and bound by RR Donnelley APS